A Note to Parents

DK READERS is a compelling program for beginning readers, designed in conjunction with leading literacy experts, including Dr. Linda Gambrell, Director of the School of Education at Clemson University. Dr. Gambrell has served on the Board of Directors of the International Reading Association and as President of the National Reading Conference.

Beautiful illustrations and superb full-color photographs combine with engaging, easy-to-read stories to offer a fresh approach to each subject in the series. Each DK READER is guaranteed to capture a child's interest while developing his or her reading skills, general knowledge, and love of reading.

The five levels of DK READERS are aimed at different reading abilities, enabling you to choose the books that are exactly right for your child:

Pre-level 1 – Learning to read
Level 1 – Beginning to read
Level 2 – Beginning to read alone
Level 3 – Reading alone
Level 4 – Proficient readers

The "normal" age at which a child begins to read can be anywhere from three to eight years old, so these levels are only a general guideline.

No matter which level you select, you can be sure that you are helping your child learn to read, then read to learn!

LONDON, NEW YORK, MUNICH,
MELBOURNE, AND DELHI

Australian Managing Editor Rosie Adams
Series Editor Deborah Lock
U.S. Editor Elizabeth Hester
Designer Adrian Saunders
Production Shivani Pandey
Photographer Leon Mead

Reading Consultant
Linda Gambrell, Ph.D.

First American Edition, 2004
04 05 06 07 08 10 9 8 7 6 5 4 3 2
Published in the United States by DK Publishing, Inc.
375 Hudson Street, New York, New York 10014

Published in Great Britain by Dorling Kindersley Limited.

A catalog record of this book is available from the
Library of Congress.

ISBN 07566-0545-8 (pbk) ISBN 0-7566-0544-X (hc)

The publisher would like to thank the National Library of Australia
for their kind permission to reproduce the image: Earle, Augustus,
1793–1838. 'Desmond, a NSW chief painted for a native dance'.
Call number: PIC T99 NK12/61 LOC Box A35,
National Library of Australia.

All other images © Dorling Kindersley Limited.
For further information see: www.dkimages.com

Models: James Mead, Luke Mead, and Bea Mead

Color reproduction by Colourscan, Singapore
Printed and bound in China by L. Rex Printing Co., Ltd.

Discover more at
www.dk.com

DK READERS

Outback Adventure
Australian Vacation

Written by Kate McLeod

DK Publishing, Inc.

James and his little brother Luke were excited about going on vacation with their parents. They would travel from their home in Perth to Broome, an Australian town in the remote area called "the outback."

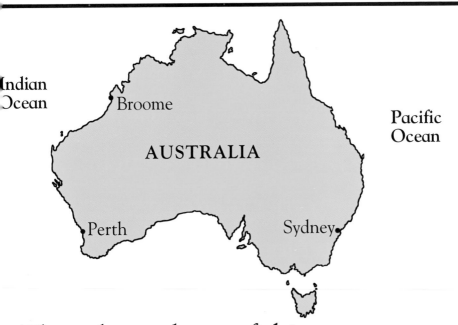

They planned to go fishing
and walking in the country.
James wanted to catch some big fish,
and Luke could not wait to go
swimming at the beach.

Broome
Broome is a town on
the northwest coast
of Australia.
It is famous for the
pearls found in the
ocean nearby.

When James, Luke, Mom, and Dad
arrived in Broome, they went to
a campground near the beach.
Right away they all raced
to the water for a swim.
Then Dad rented a boat
to go fishing.
James was lucky—
he caught four fish.

Dad lit a campfire to cook the fish
for dinner.
They were delicious!

At the beach, the boys discovered giant footprints in the rocks.
"I think it's a dinosaur's footprint," said James excitedly.
"I found one, too!" cried Luke.
"It might be from a Megalosauropus (Me-ga-luh-SORE-uh-pus)," said Mom.

"They lived in northern Australia."
The Megalosauropus were
carnivores, which means
they ate meat.

Fossils

Over millions of
years, the bones
and footprints
of dinosaurs
turn to rock.
Those rocks are
known as fossils.

The next day, the whole family went walking in the "bush"—the Australian word for "countryside." Luke discovered two giant mounds of earth.

They were enormous termite nests.
"Wow," said Luke.
"Just imagine how many termites
live in these huge nests."
"Thousands," replied James.
"They are like termite apartment
buildings."

Termites
Termites are small
insects that feed on
wood and plants.
They build giant
nests above the
ground during
the wet season.

The boys climbed over some rocks
and found a cave.
Inside the cave, there were figures
painted on the rocks.
The paintings were made with
red, yellow, and white clay.

The colored clay showed pictures of people hunting.
"These were probably painted thousands of years ago by Australian Aborigines," explained Mom.

Aborigines
Aborigines have lived in Australia for thousands of years. Early Aborigines hunted animals and gathered berries and plants for food.

The next day, the family went
to a beautiful beach in Broome.
James and Luke saw some horses
and asked if they could have a ride.
After climbing into the saddles,
James and Luke rode with the owners
through the water and on the beach.
At the end of their ride they saw
other riders.

"Look!" said Luke.

"Those people are riding camels."

"That must be a bumpy ride!"

replied James.

It was raining the next day, so the family visited the pearling museum. They found out about the history of pearl diving around Broome. They saw the old costumes that pearl divers used to wear, and James got to hold an oyster shell.

Metal helmet

Diving suit

Divers used metal helmets to help
them breathe deep under water.
"They look very heavy," said Luke.
"It must be hard to swim with them
on," James agreed.

James asked Dad about pearls. "Oysters grow deep under the water on the ocean floor," said Dad. "Divers jump off boats and swim down deep to collect the shells. When they break open the oyster shells, they look for pearls inside."

Oysters

When a piece of sand gets into the shell, the oyster coats the sand with layers of skin. They harden to make a pearl.

Mom took James and Luke
to a muddy beach to find crabs.
The crabs live in burrows under
the sand and in the rocks.

They come out to find food
on the beach.
When a big crab came out,
James caught it with a hook.
He was careful to stay away
from its strong claws.

The next day, James and Luke went
to an outback station, or ranch.
It was a huge cattle station,
as big as a city.

James met a boy named Pablo,
whose family lived at the station.
James and Pablo went to watch
jackaroos, or cowboys,
rounding up the cattle.

Station

Stations are large
farms, or ranches,
in outback Australia.
Sheep and cattle are
kept on stations, and
horses are used to
round up cattle.

James and Pablo had lots of fun
exploring the station together.
At the river, they used the soft
bark from paperbark
trees to build boats.

They raced the paperbark
boats down the river.

In the afternoon, James and his family went on a long walk through the bush around the station. It was hot, so they found a billabong, or pool, and jumped in for a swim.

Colorful butterflies
fluttered around
the billabong.
"That one looks like
a rainbow," said Luke.

James, Luke, and their parents spent the next day at the Broome Bird Observatory.
The observatory is where scientists catch and count birds so they can find out how they behave and where they fly.

Hundreds of birds
More than 200 species of birds visit northern Australia every year.
They migrate from all over the world.

James and Luke watched the scientists catching the birds with netting.
James was even allowed to hold one of the young birds.

On the last day of the trip,
the family went for a sightseeing
flight in a helicopter.
They flew over massive rocks called
the Bungle Bungles, or Purnululu—
the Aboriginal name.

"I wish we could stay!" said James. Mom replied, "We'll have to come back soon for more adventures."

Outback facts

Australia is a big country. Not many people live outside the main cities. Large areas of land where few people live are called the outback. Usually it is hot, dry, and dusty in the outback, but when it rains, green grasses and leaves appear, and the wildflowers bloom.

A station is a large farm in the outback with thousands of cattle and sheep.

In Australia, people who work with the cattle on the stations are called jackaroos. Jackaroos ride horses or motorbikes to round up the cattle. On some large stations, they use helicopters.

Billabongs are beautiful pools that are found in the outback. They are often surrounded by gum trees and bushes, and are usually close to rivers.